I SURRENDER NOVENA

WILLIAMS MARK

ABOUT SURRENDER NOVENA

The Surrender Novena originates from Fr. Dolindo Ruotolo (1882-1970), a Servant of God and potential saint. Fr. Dolindo, nicknamed "Mary's little old man," experienced significant suffering throughout his life, including a decade of paralysis before his death. He, alongside Padre Pio, a spiritual director and friend, shared words and prayers encouraging surrender to Christ and embodying His love in our interactions. During the nine-day novena, we reflect on the words Jesus revealed to Fr. Dolindo, urging us to surrender everything and trust completely in Him.

When to engage in the Surrender Novena?

Turn to the Surrender Novena whenever faced with challenges in handling matters independently or struggling to relinquish worries, doubts, or suffering to God.

Reasons for Praying the Surrender Novena:

This prayer, bestowed by Jesus through Fr. Dolindo Ruotolo, holds profound power. Just as Jesus met Fr. Dolindo in pain, suffering, and doubt, we too encounter Jesus through these words. The novena serves to humble ourselves, acknowledging our inability to manage everything alone and relying on Jesus for care. Through surrender, we redirect our focus from self to Jesus.

How to Pray the Surrender Novena

Time needed 5 minute

1. Begin with the sign of the cross.
   In the name of the Father, and of the Son, and of the Holy Spirit, Amen.

2. Listen or read Jesus' words to Fr. Dolindo Ruotolo each day, reflecting on His guidance for peace and comfort over the next nine days and beyond.

3. Repeat the surrender refrain 10 times.
   "O Jesus, I surrender myself to You, take care of everything!"

4. Conclude with a prayer from Servant of God Fr. Dolindo Ruotolo.
   "Mother, I am yours now and forever. Through you and with you, I always want to belong completely to Jesus."

5. Finally, end with the sign of the cross.

In the name of the Father, and of the Son, and of the Holy Spirit, Amen.

SURRENDER NOVENA

_Day 1

Why complicate your minds with worries? Entrust your affairs to me, and serenity will prevail. Truthfully, genuine, unwavering surrender to me resolves difficulties and brings about the desired effects.

Repeat 10 times: "O Jesus, I surrender myself to you, take care of everything!"

SURRENDER NOVENA — DAY 2

Surrendering to me doesn't involve fretting, becoming distressed, or losing hope. It's not about anxiously praying for me to follow you and transform your worries into prayers. Truly surrendering means refraining from worry, nervousness, and the desire to contemplate consequences.

It's akin to the confusion children feel when asking their mother for assistance, yet simultaneously attempting to handle their needs independently, hindering their mother's efforts. Surrender involves calmly shutting the eyes of the soul, diverting from thoughts of tribulation, and entrusting yourself to my care, saying, "You take care of it."

Repeat 10 times: "O Jesus, I surrender myself to you, take care of everything!"

SURRENDER NOVENA _ Day 3

When a soul, burdened with both spiritual and material needs, turns to me, gazes at me, and says, "You take care of it," then closes its eyes and rests, numerous things unfold. Often, in pain, you pray for my intervention but insist on it aligning with your preferences. Instead of turning to me, you expect me to conform to your ideas. You resemble not patients asking a doctor for healing but patients dictating how the doctor should proceed. Refrain from such behavior; instead, pray in the manner I taught you in the Our Father: "Hallowed be thy Name," seeking glorification in your need. "Thy kingdom come," desiring alignment with your kingdom in us and the world. "Thy will be done on Earth as it is in Heaven," meaning, in our need, let decisions be made according to your wisdom for our temporal and eternal lives. If you sincerely say, "Thy will be done," synonymous with "You take care of it," I will intervene with my omnipotence and resolve the most challenging situations.

Repeat 10 times: "O Jesus, I surrender myself to you, take care of everything!"

SURRENDER NOVENA —
Day 4

If you witness the growth of evil instead of its weakening, don't be troubled. Close your eyes and express with faith: "Thy will be done, You take care of it." I assure you that I will attend to it, intervening like a doctor and performing miracles when necessary. If you observe a deterioration in the condition of the sick, remain calm, close your eyes, and say, "You take care of it." I affirm that I will handle it, and my loving intervention surpasses any medicine.

Repeat 10 times: "O Jesus, I surrender myself to you, take care of everything!"

SURRENDER NOVENA _ Day 5

When I guide you along a path different from what you perceive, I will prepare you. I will carry you in my arms, allowing you to find yourself, like children who peacefully sleep in their mother's embrace, on the opposite side of the river. Your distress stems from your reason, thoughts, excessive worry, and the strong desire to independently address your troubles.

Repeat 10 times: "O Jesus, I surrender myself to you, take care of everything"

SURRENDER NOVENA __ Day 6

In your restless state, you seek to judge, control, and manage everything, relying on human strength or, worse, placing trust in people themselves. This impedes my words and perspectives. I earnestly desire your surrender to assist you, and I experience distress seeing you so agitated. Satan attempts to provoke this agitation, pulling you away from my protection and pushing you into the realm of human initiative. Therefore, place your trust solely in me, find rest in me, and surrender everything to me.

Repeat 10 times: "O Jesus, I surrender myself to you, take care of everything"

SURRENDER NOVENA __ Day 7

Miracles unfold in proportion to your complete surrender to me and your selflessness. I bestow abundant graces when you are in profound poverty. No rational individual or thinker has ever performed miracles, not even among the saints. Divine works occur when one surrenders to God. Cease contemplating it, as your sharp mind finds it challenging to overlook evil and trust in me without focusing on yourself. Apply this approach to all your needs, and you will witness continuous, silent miracles. I will handle things—I assure you of this.

Repeat 10 times: "O Jesus, I surrender myself to you, take care of everything!"

SURRENDER NOVENA — Day 8

Shut your eyes and allow yourself to be carried by the flowing stream of my grace. Close your eyes, dismissing thoughts of the present and turning away from the future as you would from temptation. Rest in me, having faith in my goodness, and I pledge, through my love, that if you declare, "You take care of it," I will handle everything—consoling, liberating, and guiding you.

Repeat 10 times: "O Jesus, I surrender myself to you, take care of everything!"

SURRENDER NOVENA _
Day 9

Maintain a constant readiness to surrender in your prayers, and you will receive immense peace and rewards, even when I bestow upon you the grace of sacrifice, repentance, and love. In the face of suffering, what does it matter? If it appears insurmountable, close your eyes and proclaim with your entire soul, "Jesus, you take care of it." Fear not; I will manage things, and in your humility, you will bless my name. Remember well, a thousand prayers cannot match a single act of surrender. There is no novena more potent than this.

Repeat 10 times: "O Jesus, I surrender myself to you, take care of everything!"

Mother, I am now and forever yours. Through you and with you, I desire to belong completely to Jesus.

Our Heavenly Father, acknowledging our numerous earthly needs, urges us to prioritize seeking Him in trust for their fulfillment according to His wisdom, as Jesus emphasizes in Matthew 6:32.

To fortify your faith through this novena and similar ones, endeavor to follow Jesus with loving obedience. This approach stands as a crucial means to strengthen your Faith. In both Matthew 13:58 and Mark 6:5, we find accounts of Jesus being limited in performing miracles in Nazareth due to the people's lack of faith.

Allow Him to work miracles within you, even if it means the significant achievement of helping you persevere with reduced anxiety in times of hardship. At the very least, you'll experience a greater peace of mind, staying in constant communication with our Lord through prayers like this novena, assured that He has your back. Ultimately, let His triumph over sin and death in His Passion become yours in a different way, manifested in the life of the world to come.

LITANY OF SURRENDERING TO GOD'S WILL

Lord, have mercy. Lord, have mercy.

Christ, have mercy. Christ, have mercy.

Lord, have mercy. Lord, have mercy.

God, the Father of Heaven, Have mercy on me.

God, the Son, Redeemer of the world, Have mercy on me.

God, the Holy Spirit, the Sanctifier, Have mercy on me.

Holy Trinity, One God, Have mercy on me.

Christ, hear me. Christ, graciously hear me.

In reverence, I yield to Your Will, O God.

In devotion, I yield to Your Will, O God.

In longing, I yield to Your Will, O God.

In anticipation, I yield to Your Will, O God.

In modesty, I yield to Your Will, O God.

In compliance, I yield to Your Will, O God.

In faith, I yield to Your Will, O God.

In candor, I yield to Your Will, O God.

In sincerity, I yield to Your Will, O God.

In openness, I yield to Your Will, O God.

In uprightness, I yield to Your Will, O God.

In dedication, I yield to Your Will, O God.

In allegiance, I yield to Your Will, O God.

In impartiality, I yield to Your Will, O God.

In strength, I yield to Your Will, O God.

In perception, I yield to Your Will, O God.

In sagacity, I yield to Your Will, O God.

In compassion, I yield to Your Will, O God.

In equity, I yield to Your Will, O God.

In steadfastness, I yield to Your Will, O God.

In self-control, I yield to Your Will, O God.

In pardon, I yield to Your Will, O God.

In empathy, I yield to Your Will, O God.

In gentleness, I yield to Your Will, O God.

In benevolence, I yield to Your Will, O God.

In intimacy, I yield to Your Will, O God.

In supplication, I yield to Your Will, O God.

In gratitude, I yield to Your Will, O God.

In admiration, I yield to Your Will, O God.

In spontaneity, I yield to Your Will, O God.

In appropriateness, I yield to Your Will, O God.

In genuineness, I yield to Your Will, O God.

In inventiveness, I yield to Your Will, O God.

In concern, I yield to Your Will, O God.

In bravery, I yield to Your Will, O God.

In tenderness, I yield to Your Will, O God.

In companionship, I yield to Your Will, O God.

In innocence, I yield to Your Will, O God.

In gentleness, I yield to Your Will, O God.

In virtue, I yield to Your Will, O God.

In tranquility, I yield to Your Will, O God.

In comprehension, I yield to Your Will, O God.

In guidance, I yield to Your Will, O God.

In wisdom, I yield to Your Will, O God.

In devotion, I yield to Your Will, O God.

In diligence, I yield to Your Will, O God.

In collaboration, I yield to Your Will, O God.

In patience, I yield to Your Will, O God.

In persistence, I yield to Your Will, O God.

In faith, I yield to Your Will, O God.

In hope, I yield to Your Will, O God.

In love, I yield to Your Will, O God.

Christ, hear me. Christ, graciously hear me.

Lamb of God, You take away the sins of the world,
Spare me, O Lord.

Lamb of God, You take away the sins of the world,
Graciously hear me, O Lord.

Lamb of God, You take away the sins of the world,
Have mercy on me.

Our Father, etc.

Let Me Pray:

Lord, Your Holy Will is, or should be, the essence of my
Christian life. Ensure that I follow Your Holy Will
in every aspect, unable to do anything outside of
Your Holy Will. Direct my entire life so that I
cannot evade Your Holy Will. May I willingly,
freely, and without complaint, despair,
presumption,

or corruption fulfill it. May I persevere until the end.
Through Jesus Christ, Our Lord. Amen.

Made in the USA
Middletown, DE
11 September 2024

60801691R00015